Sitting in Pictures

Vision Meditations for Addiction Recovery
by Peoples of the Earth

Illustrations by Christine Sundly,
Menominee Nation

SittinginPictures.org

ISBN: 978-1-934569-15-3

Library of Congress Control Number:
2012937481

Being Indian and being spiritual has the same meaning. Spirituality is our gift from the Great One. This day I vow to walk the Red Road. ~*White Bison, The Red Road to Wellbriety*

Our gratitude to :
> ~AA Big Book *(Alcoholic's Anonymous)*
> ~CDA First Edition *(Chemically Dependent Anonymous)*
> ~NA Basic Text *(Narcotic's Anonymous)*
> ~Red Road *(The Red Road to Wellbriety, In The Native American Way)*

Introduction

Sitting in Pictures,* is an amazing Hopi tradition whereby one practices visualizing a harmonious reality, sitting in that reality, and allowing it to manifest. The practice is used to promote harmony and unity, heal the self, the family and the community, and foster an awareness of Creator. Not confined to the Hopi alone, "Sitting in Pictures" is known by other names with various peoples. Indeed, the vision quest of Native Americans may be a form of Sitting In Pictures, the Dreamtime of the Aborigines is an ever expanding form of reality, the reliefs from Göbekli Tepe could be a form of "pictures" to enhance the spiritual life and even so-called modern psychology's "creative visualization" is, no doubt, a similar endeavor.

Traditional meditation books for addiction recovery have been based on wise words that stir the soul, but originate from the head. Our approach is different. Each page consists of three things;

- a 12 Step Principle of Recovery
- a Sacred Image to "sit" in
- a Quote or Adage from an Elder, Shaman, or a Tribal Tradition

It is easier for many of us to grasp the healing message of a meditation if we approach it by creating a door to the reality in which we heal. This doorway is the daily image from *Sitting in Pictures*. Our meditation book humbly attempts to draw healing, wisdom, and guidance from other realms--for those of us who don't live so much in the intellect but dwell in the soul of our planet.

* *Described in Blue Highways by William Least Heat Moon*

Timekeeping

Various calendar systems around the world were created to mark celestial events, seasons, agricultural dates and religious celebrations. They typically chart events placed in time such as cycles around the sun, (solar calendar), cycles of the moon (lunation) or other cycles based on the movements of planets, stars, and even galaxies. Some calendars mark cycles of consciousness and development having little to do with solar years and more to do with humanity's spirituality. For instance, the *Tzolkin* (*Sacred Round*) calendar of the Mayan Day Keepers completes a 260 day (9 month) cycle.

Sitting in Pictures is loosely based on that of the *Tzolkin* time frame, the gestation period for a human being.

Readers may use the meditations randomly, as the Spirit guides them, or begin with the first meditation closest to the Summer Solstice, Fall Equinox, Winter

Solstice, or Spring Equinox. Synchronization with today's calendar is not necessary to use this book. We trust that every reader will bring their own guidance on where they wish to begin their healing meditations.

We have learned from the world's most advanced timekeepers that every moment of every day should be honored for the sacred purpose it is meant to serve. We hope you honor your clean and sober days, in this modest attempt to bring you sacred drawings used in our shared healing and sobriety.

Sitting
In Pictures

Summer Solstice

Beginning with our Best

"How can I best serve Thee - Thy will (not mine) be done." ~AA Big Book, p 85

Toltec: The Fourth Agreement

Always Do Your Best ~Don Miguel Ruiz, Naugle of the Eagle Knight Lineage--Mexico

Summertime

Losing the Self

Does what I gain by lying really balance out the integrity I lose? ~*CDA First Edition. P 54*

Lose your temper and you lose a friend; lie and you lose yourself. ~*Hopi*

Summertime

Looking Back

How long does it take to clear away the wreckage of our past?

In the Northwest region of the U.S., Native Americans have a special saying:

"How long does it take to clear a landslide?"

Answer:

"One rock at a time."

Summertime

Mind Changers

We of CDA do not make distinctions in the
recovery process based on any particular
substance, believing that the addictive
compulsive usage of chemicals is
the core of our disease and the
use of any mood-changing
chemical will result in relapse.
~*CDA First Edition, Intro*

But we do have the power to overcome this
mind changer (alcohol). One way is just not to
drink it. If you never drink it, you won't have
to enter the testing time. ~*White Bison, The
Red Road to Wellbriety. P J*

Summertime

Walk a Good Path

Walk the walk, don't just talk the talk.

Talking about a path is not walking that path.
Thinking about life is not living. ~Lao-Tzo, A
Path and A Practice

Summertime

Great Spirit

I simply had to believe in a Spirit of the Universe, who knew neither time nor limitation. ~AA Big Book, P 10

The Great Spirit is in all things, he is in the air we breathe. ~Big Thunder (Bedagi-Wabanaki Algonquin)

Summertime

Movement

If you are not going forward, you are going backward.

Movement is wellness. *~Quoted from a Tsuutina First Nation tribal woman.*

Summertime

Give Without Strings

You received without cost, now give without charge. ~*Walk Softly and Carry a Big Book*

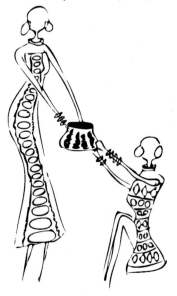

"Mahala" is the traditional African practice which teaches us to give to our fellows without expectation. Not everything needs to be done for money or gain. ~*Ubuntu Culture*

Summertime

What is Missing?

What was missing in my program was the spiritual: the active presence of a Power greater than myself. ~*CDA First Edition P. 148*

Creator would not be complete without YOU!
~*Keith Lytle, First Nations*

Summertime

Following the old ways

When an old-timer dies, a library is lost.

Today, what is important for us to realize is that the old sacred ways are correct, and that if we do not follow them we will be lost and without a guide. ~*Thomas Yellowtail, Crow*

Summertime

Life is an Instrument

How should two people treat each other if
they both know   God? Like a
musician touching   his violin
with utmost   care.
~Hafiz

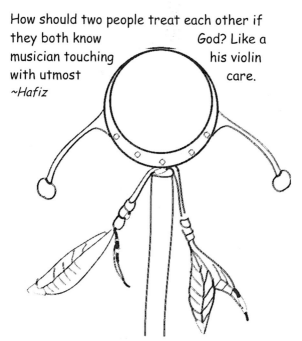

Life is an instrument and we have lost the
ability to play it. People live but they are not
alive. We must use life and play it like an
instrument and make beautiful music. ~Credo
Mutwa, Zulu Sangoma

Summertime

Conscious Contact

Take my will and my life. Guide me in my recovery. Show me how to live. *~Narcotics Anonymous Third Step Prayer*

Might I behold thee, Might I know thee, Might I consider thee, Might I understand thee, O Lord of the universe. *~Inca Song*

Summertime

Hand in Hand

The joy of the fellowship is that *we* work together, hand in hand with one another and with a Higher Power of our own understanding. ~*Conscious Contact, Feb 9*

The people who gather are a tribe not of blood but of spirit, for all are born into it. We are bound together by our desire to live in peace, to be in the cathedral of nature, and to heal ourselves through union with the earthly mother and heavenly father. ~*Rainbow Gathering*

Summertime

Loose Tongues

Gossip, rumors, backbiting, loose tongues, verbal altercations: sometimes AA meetings are like the corner bar, without the alcohol.

If a bad word comes in your ear and then comes out of your mouth, it will go someplace and hurt somebody. If I did that, that hurt would come back twice as hard on me.
~ *Wallace Black Elk, Lakota*

Summertime

Sacred is Sober

Though they knew they must help other alcoholics if they would remain sober, that motive became secondary. *~Big Book, p 159*

Drinking is not Indian. *~National native Alcohol and Drug Abuse Program, Canada*

Summertime

God Cannot be Measured

Look for your Higher Power everywhere,
because that's where your Higher Power is.
~Walk Softly and Carry a Big Book

The dreaming as we refer to--it is the spirit,
and that is something we all know cannot be
measured or confined. No beginning, no end.
That is what "The Dreaming" is, the spirit.
~Harold Hunt, Australia

Summertime

You are not Alone

This is a "*We*" Program.

Wa'ce Waki'ya! "I am embracing relatives all around us.!"~*Lakota Sioux Elders as told to Richard Voss, in the Journal Quadrant*

Summertime

Following the Ways of Sober Ones

You don't have to like your sponsor. You only have to want what they have--sobriety.

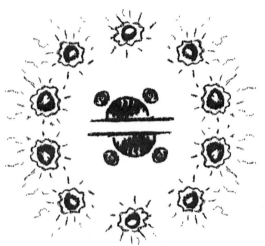

We all know we have history and our culture. Our Elders gave this all to us. Everything around us is affecting us and going through this program of AA; it gives you life and gives everything back to you. *a "traditional" Aboriginal man at the 1999 Darwin National Aboriginal Network Conference*

Summertime

Charity

We asked God to help us show them the same tolerance, pity, and patience that we would cheerfully grant a sick friend. *~Big Book, P. 67*

An ancient Mayan prayer asks for the gift of understanding.

Start your Day Quietly

When you start the day with quiet meditation, you create a consciousness of serenity and peace. At anytime during the day you can bring your mind back to this moment. *~Pocket Sponsor, Day Fourteen/5:00 AM*

Oh Great Spirit, Let me walk in beauty, and make my eyes ever behold the red and purple sunsets. *~Ojibwa Prayer*

Summertime

Seeing our Way into Recovery

If your only tool is a hammer, everything you see will be a nail.

We don't see things as they are. We see things as we are. ~*Talmudic Saying*

Summertime

The Voice of Higher Power

Try to listen sober. Your ears work better that way. ~*Walk Softly and Carry a Big Book*

Speak to an energy that rises up in one's soul and dances in magical ways to ignite a passion that carries that individual in a direction by which they are able to find the voice of their Higher Power within. ~*Leah, Spokane*

Summertime

Misuse of Powerful Forces

Am I Higher Powered today?

It is this sharing that must be considered with great care by the Elders and the medicine people who carry the Sacred Trusts, so that no harm may come to people through ignorance and misuse of these powerful forces. ~*Resolution of the Fifth Annual Meetings of the Traditional Elders Circle, 1980*

Summertime

Understanding

You may not understand why you are chemically dependent, but rest assured there is a purpose in your cycle of sobriety. *~Pocket Sponsor, Day Three 3pm*

If you understand, things are just as they are; if you do not understand, things are just as they are. *~Zen Proverb*

Summertime

The Journey

Recovery is a journey, not a destination. May
your journey be long.

May you always walk in Beauty. *~Ancient Prayer*

Summertime

Service is Sacred

...our sometimes smoke-filled, coffee-filled, talk-filled clubs, meetings, and social gatherings are the basis for a lot more than laughter—they add up to a major part of our recovery. *~May 29, Day By Day*

True happiness comes only to those who dedicate their lives to the service of others. *~Code of Discipline from International Aboriginal Ministries*

Summertime

Spiritual Awakening

Don't go to sleep before your Spirtual Awakening.

Before spiritual awakening...work steps, make coffee, carry the message. After spiritual awakening...keep working steps, keep making coffee, keep carrying the message. *~Zen for the 12 Steps*

Summertime

Speak up in Meetings

You don't *have* to share in meetings, but it might be a good idea.

Beware of the man who does not talk, and the dog that does not bark. ~*Cheyenne*

Summertime

The Present Moment

Yesterday's history, tomorrow's a mystery,
the present is all we have.

Our true home is in the present moment. The
miracle is not to walk on water,

The miracle is to walk on the green earth in
the present moment. *~Thich Nhat Ranh*

Summertime

Prayer is the Key

We sought through prayer and meditation...
~Step Eleven

"ةليللا لفقلا و راهنلل حاتفملا تلاصلا"
Prayer is the Key of the Day and the Lock of
the Night. ~Aramaic (language of Jesus)

Heart of Sky

In NA, staying clean has to come first. We realize that we cannot use drugs and live. *~NA Basic Text, p 19*

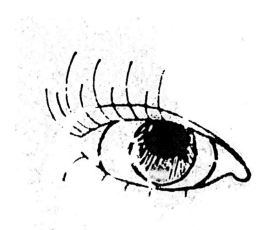

What fills the eye fills the heart. *~Gaelic: An rud a líonas an tsúil líonann sé an croí.*

Whole People

This is a Three-fold disease: physical, mental, and spiritual.

The Native Peoples saw a being as a Whole person: mental, emotional, spiritual and physical--all one. Their equivalent of "doctors" were also usually Spiritual Leaders, and they treated the Whole Person. *~Star spider dancing*

Summertime

Choose

Choose your life; don't let it choose you.
~Walk Softly and Carry A Big Book

Do not vacillate or you will be left in between doing something, having something and being nothing. *~Ethiopia*

Summertime

World as Two Things

We want to stop drinking and using and we want to drink and use.

In our minds we are two, good and evil. With our eyes we see two things, things that are fair and things that are ugly.... We have the right hand that strikes and makes for evil, and we have the left hand full of kindness, near the heart. *~Eagle Chief (Letakos-Lesa) Pawnee*

Summertime

Guidance

Step 11. Sought through prayer and meditation to improve our conscious contact with God *as we understood Him,* praying only for knowledge of His will for us and the power to carry that out.

Pray for guidance. Many things are not known.
~*Sven Haakanson, Jr., Alutiiq People of the Kodiac Archipelago, Alaska Peninsula*

Summertime

The Silence of Words

God gave us two ears and one mouth for a reason.

TAO cannot be covered by words or by silence. In the state which is neither speed nor silence, its special awareness may be caught. ~*Chuan Tzu*

Summertime

How to Tell your Story

Tell us what it was like, what happened, and what it is like now.

Clearly the Dreaming is many things in one.......
among them a kind of narrative of things that
once happened; a kind of charter of things
that still happen; and a kind of Logos or
principle of order transcending everything
significant for (Aboriginal) man. *~WEH
Stanner 1979*

Summertime

Open Hearts

Everyone becomes a teacher in the program if we simply open our minds and hearts.

If we learn to open our hearts, anyone, including the people who drive us crazy, can be our teacher. ~Pema Chödrön

Summertime

Bridge to the Divine

Some of us had already walked far over the Bridge of Reason toward the desired shore of faith. ~*Big Book, p 53*

Runes are like a bridge between the self and divine--a gateway symbol. It indicates there is work to be done inside and outside one's self. Look back before entering, let go of the past, then step through the gateway. ~*Book of Runes*

Summertime

Spiritual Matters

In Spiritual matters,
the Spiritual matters.

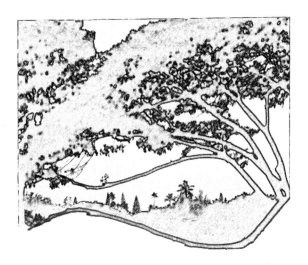

Spiritual matters are difficult to explain because you must live with them in order to fully understand them ~*Thomas Yellowtail, CROW*

Summertime

Sitting in Purpose

To every thing there is a season, and a time to every purpose under the heaven. ~*King James Bible*

Each life has a purpose to mold and to make; we all need the gift of our Brother, the Snake. ~*Faye Clark Haynes - Rainbow in the West*

Summertime

Bad Spirit

It is bad spirit that takes up residence in us with addiction. Going for treatment is a natural process and getting rid of bad spirit is a supernatural process.

There is no distinction between the natural and the supernatural. Where would the ancestral spirits reside if not in the crune, the cloud, the cave, the buffalo, and the tree? ~*Mahdoma Drgara tribal Elder, West Africa*

Summertime

Laughing is Good Medicine

Why shouldn't we laugh? *~Big Book, p 132*

We learn best while laughing. *~Native Storyteller, Terry Tefya*

Summertime

Story Telling

We share what it was like, what happened,
and what it is like now.

Stories have minds of their own.
They yearn to be told. Untold stories feel
forsaken. If neglected too long, the stories
become belligerent and plot retaliation. *~East
Indian Folk Tales p 12*

Summertime

Health Within

We are only as healthy as our honesty.

OLA MAI ILOKO MAI.
      Health comes from within. ~*Hawaiiana*

Summertime

Awakening (Step 12)

Having had a spiritual awakening as a result of these steps...

Your vision will become clear only when you look into your heart ...Who looks outside, dreams. Who looks inside, awakens. ~Carl Jung

Summertime

Listen

Listen to your heart often, God lives there.
~Walk Softly and Carry a Big Book

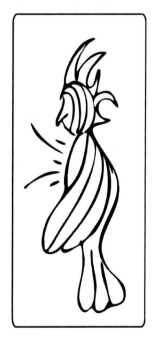

Knock on the sky and listen to the sound! *~Zen Saying*

Summertime

Stories that Dance

Each individual, in the personal stories
describes in his own language and from his
own point of
view the way he
established his
relationship
with God.
  ~Big Book, P 29

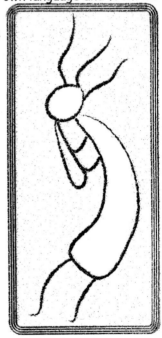

What do the stories do when they are not
being told? *(they dance in-between)* ~Lakota
Proverb

Summertime

Life on Life's Terms

Recovery does not guarantee us freedom
from living life on life's terms. In Narcotics
Anonymous we can learn to accept the reality
of   life, which sometimes brings us
illness or injury.
~Mark E, Toronto

Cattle die, kindred die,
Every man is mortal.
But the good name will never fade
Of one who has lived honorably. ~attributed to
Odin. Ancient Nordic Spirituality by Douglas "Dag"
Rossman

Summertime

Smoky Mirror

We need our sponsors to tell us the truth because we often only see ourselves through a smoky mirror.

Bu mhath an sgàthan sùil caraid. A friend's eye is a good looking-glass. ~*Gaelic Indigenousness: Native Gaelic Language Sayings*

Summertime

Do not Walk Alone

We feel we are on the Broad Highway, walking hand in hand with the Spirit of the Universe.
~Big Book, P75

After "Pachakuti" (period of cleansing), a hole in the fabric of time will appear, and those who have prepared for it will be able to walk through it and into their luminous bodies.
~Peruvian shamans of the Q'ero line

Summertime

Our Side of the Street

We stay on our side of the street. Keep the focus on ourself. We do not take another's inventory.

Whatever we sow we will simultaneously reap for ourselves. We must be accountable for our own actions. ~*Spirited Wolf*

Summertime

It's Day

We celebrate our first day of recovery by calling it a "birthday" because that is the day we are reborn.

"its-day his-being-born," the phrase still used for "birthday." ~POPOL VUH:, THE MAYAN BOOK OF THE DAWN OF LIFE (C) Copyright 1985, Dennis Tedlock

Summertime

Indomitable Spirit

The unselfishness of these men {...}, the entire absence of profit motive, and their community spirit, is indeed inspiring to one who has labored long and wearily in this alcoholic field. *~The Doctor's Opinion*

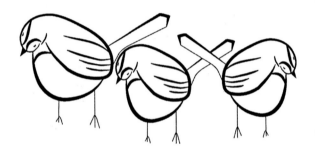

We learned to be patient observers like the owl. We learned cleverness from the crow, and courage from the jay, who will attack an owl ten times its size to drive it off its territory. But above all of them ranked the chickadee because of its indomitable spirit. *~Tom Brown, Jr., The Tracker*

Summertime

Winds of Pity

NO self-pity. The moment this emotion strikes, do something nice for someone less fortunate than you.

Sometimes I go about pitying myself, and all along, my soul is being blown by great winds across the sky. ~Ojibway saying

Summertime

The Thirst

Hope for the best but prepare for the thirst.

Good as drink is, it ends in thirst. Dá fheabhas é an t-ól is é an tart n dheireadh. ~*Gaelic*

Summertime

In Judgment

Do not condemn the judgment of another
because it differs from your own. You may
both be wrong.

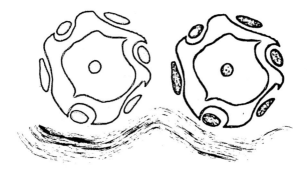

Do not judge your neighbor until you walk two
moons in his moccasins. *~Cheyenne*

Summertime

Gives Strength

Our founders give strength to us because they paved the way. It is they who speak with the Heart of Sky and Earth.

...make my guilt vanish,
   my grandmothers, grandfathers,
   and however many souls of the dead there may be, you who speak with the Heart of Sky and Earth, may all of you together give strength. *~Popol Vuh, Andres Xiloj daykeeper from Momostenango, (Guatemala)*

Summertime

Patience

We wish you the gift of a slow recovery.

Have patience. Some things cannot be rushed.
~Nora Marks Dauenhauer, tlingit People,
Southeast Alaska

Summertime

Meditate

After all, no man can build a house until he first envisions a plan for it. Well, meditation is like that, too; it helps to envision our spiritual objective before we try to move toward it. ~*Twelve & Twelve, p 98*

Listen to guidance and follow the guidance given to your heart. Expect guidance to come in many forms: in dreams, in times of quiet solitude and in the words and deeds of wise elders and friends. ~*The Sacred Tree*

Summertime

Connect

An addict may be helpless at times, but never hopeless as long as they keep a phone list of people in the fellowship.

Living here in my Grandmother's Country is changing me in so many ways. I feel a lot more connected to this as a sober person. Living here in the bush I feel the presence of the land much more strongly. ~Marilyn, Kiola Beach, Australia

Wanting

Plan plans, not results.

Do not be always wanting everything to turn out as you think it should, but rather as God pleases, then you will be undisturbed and thankful in your prayer. ~*Abba Nilus, Desert Father*

Summertime

Our Greatest Enemy

So our troubles, we think, are basically of our own making. ~*Big Book, p 62*

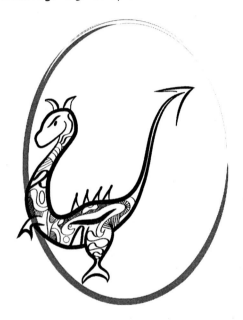

I seek strength not to be superior to my brothers, but to be able to fight my greatest enemy, myself. ~*Traditional Native American Prayer*

Summertime

Medicine Keepers

We've learned in NA that we can apply spiritual principals to help us get through these difficult times. When we admit that we are powerless, we can accept our illness and any necessary medical treatment. *~Mark E, Toronto*

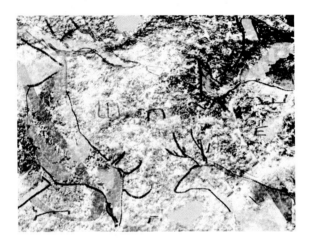

......Objects can be "Medicine" for a Being. Some things are "Medicine" for emotions, or spirit, or mind, or body, some for all four. Herbs too are "Medicine", as well as modern medicines. *~Star Spider Dancing*

Summertime

Hearth Groups

Many meetings, many chances; few meetings, few chances; no meetings, no chances.

No culture can live if it attempts to be exclusive. ~Mahatma Gandhi

Summertime

Fellowship of the Spirit

Every new alcoholic looks for this spirit among us and is immensely relieved when he finds we are not witch burners. ~*Big Book, p 103*

It is time to speak your Truth. Create your community. Be good to each other. And do not look outside yourself for the leader. This could be a good time! ~*Oraibi, Arizona Hopi Nation*

Summer Solstice

Twinkle of Time

Time is a gift, not a threat. ~*Daily Reflections*

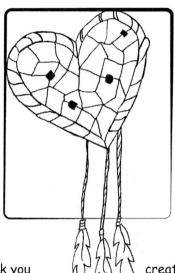

We thank you   creator for
your Love and   forgiveness
and for our Love for each other; and for you,
our dear brothers and sisters, and for the
bright light of the ancestral fire that
continues to light the pathway for Walela, in
this twinkle of time. ~*Love Walela.*

Summertime

Different Drugs-Different Snakes

Marijuana controls our lives! We lose interest in all else; our dreams go up in smoke. Ours is a progressive illness often leading us to addictions to other drugs, including alcohol.
~*Life With Hope, p. xi*

If a snake bites your neighbor, you too are in danger. ~*Swahili Wisdom*

Summertime

Everything is Here

Don't fight drink, strengthen sobriety. ~*Walk Softly and Carry A Big Book*

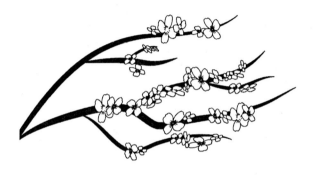

Nothing to seek...everything is here. If we try to get rid of something, it will naturally remain. If we try to weaken a habit, it will naturally remain strong. ~*Lao-Tzo, A Path and A Practice, Chapter 36*

Summertime

Cease Fighting

And we have ceased fighting anything or anyone - even alcohol. ~*Big Book, p 84*

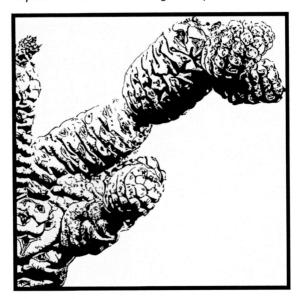

Nee-Mee-Poo/hinmatowyalßhtqit: I am tired of fighting.... from where the sun now stands, I will fight no more. ~*Chief Joseph, Nez Perce (Nimiputimt)*

Summertime

Fall Equinox

Assuming

Don't assume evil motives.

Toltec: The Third Agreement

*Don't Make Assumptions ~Don Miguel Ruiz,
Naugle of the Eagle Knight Lineage—Mexico*

Harvest Time

Telling All

The way it was put to me, "Until someone in AA knows everything you know about yourself, you are nowhere. The result is nil until you tell it all and let go absolutely." *~Barefoot Bob, barefootsworld.net*

Bu mhath an sgàthan sùil caraid.
A friend's eye is a good looking-glass. *~Gaelic Indigenousness: Native Gaelic Language Sayings And The Decolonisation Of Anglo Peoples*

Harvest Time

Oldtimers are Elders

As an old timer in Alcoholics Anonymous used to say, "You've got to accept it just as it is!" He'd go on, saying that if the acceptance was real and true, the letting go would just happen. ~Anne, Powerfully Recovered.com

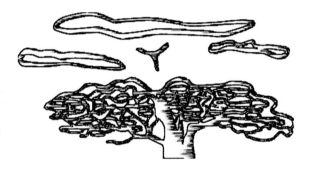

When our elders do speak, they teach us through symbol and story. They hear what we cannot hear and they see what we cannot see. The speak about knowledge that we cannot obtain on our own. ~Adama Doumbia, Naomi Doumbia, the way of the elders: West African spirituality & tradition

Harvest Time

In their One Face

Tradition One: Personal recovery depends on AA unity.

In unity: This is chiquihunam uach, "in-their-one face," an idiom {...}. as hunam quiuach, "in agreement," and {...} as hunamah uach, "to make friends." ~*Popol Vuh; the Mayan Book of the Dawn of Life* , Dennis Tedlock

Harvest Time

The Winds are Listening

As soon as we admitted the possible existence of a Creative Intelligence, a Spirit of the Universe underlying the totality of things, we began to be possessed of a new sense of power and direction. *~Big Book, p 46*

There is one God looking down on us all. We are all the children of one God. The sun, the darkness, the winds are all listening to what we have to say. *~Geronimo*

Harvest Time

Be Present

We can reach up and in and hold on and hang
in there. If we just stop... We can climb up
from that dark hole. And be here. Be present.
Be awake for the next miracle." *~Ruth Fishel,
Hang in 'Til the Miracle Happens*

The present is holy ground. *~Alfred North
Whitehead quoted in Teaching Your Children
About God, by David Wolpe*

Harvest Time

Great Spirit-Like

Rather than put a label on yourself as Christian, Jew, Muslim, Buddhist, or whatever, instead make a commitment to be Christ-like, God-like, Buddha-like and Mohammed-like. ~Dr. Wayne Dryer

Today I strive to be 'Great Spirit-Like.'

Harvest Time

The Voice of Addiction

The Babbler may begin to talk in your head, "You're stupid; they're stupid; who wants sobriety; boy, is this dumb." Babbler is not the voice of Higher Power. It is the voice of addiction.

~The Pocket Sponsor, Day Ten/12:00 AM

Day and night cannot dwell together.
~Duwamish

Harvest Time

Can You Listen?

Did you actually listen to the last person that tried to help you?

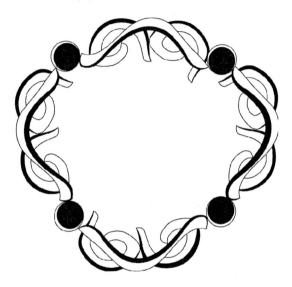

If you wish peace, friendship and quietness, listen, look and be silent. (Mas math leat sith, càirdeas agud cluain, èisd, faic is fuirich sàmhach.) ~Gaelic Indigenousness: Native Gaelic Language Sayings

Harvest Time

In the Image of God

Be humble and you will not stumble.

The law that says man was created in the image of God, I don't think that's true, I mean not totally true, because the deer and bears and the eagles and the fish have every right to say the same thing... ~Tom Porter, Mohawk. Profiles in Wisdom by Steven McFadden

Harvest Time

Right Place

It has been said, "If your stomach's all tied up in knots, you're probably in the right place." ~Narcotics Anonymous Welcome Pamphlet

The heart of healing is spirit presented--they must be in the right place of heart connection. ~Uqualla (crossingworlds.com)

Harvest Time

Higher Power

Higher Power means different things to different people. To some of us, it is a God of an organized religion; to others, it is a state of being commonly called spirituality. Some of us believe in no deity; a Higher Power may be the strength gained from being a part of, and caring for, a community of others. *~Marijuana Anonymous' book Life With Hope, p 7*

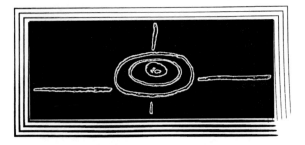

One thing we know, which the white man may one day discover, our God is the same God. You may think now that you own Him as you wish to own our land; but you cannot. He is the God of man; and His compassion is equal for the red man and the white. *~Chief Seattle*

Harvest Time

Wolf and Bear

Despite all we can say, many who are real alcoholics are not going to believe they are in that class. By every form of self-deception and experimentation, they will try to prove themselves exceptions to the rule, therefore nonalcoholic. *~Big Book, p 31*

I ran from the wolf and ran into a bear.
~Russian Proverb

Harvest Time

Worry

"Don't you worry none, just take it like it comes, one day at a time." ~Song, One Day at a Time

The foolish man lies awake all night thinking of his many problems. When the morning comes he is worn out, and his trouble is just as it was. ~Hávamál st. 23 (Nordic)

Harvest Time

What Creator Gives

Right place, right time. *~NA saying*

Remember: If the Creator put it there, it is in the right place. The soul would have no rainbow if the eyes had no tears." *~An Indian Chief, 1876*

Harvest Time

Beyond Fear

Fear not that your life shall come to an end but rather that it shall never have a beginning. *~Walk Softly and Carry a Big Book*

There are deep springs within each of us and within them, there is a sound—the sound of the deep calling to the deep. The time for rebirth is now. *~Australian Aboriginal Teaching*

Harvest Time

You are our Family

We are clean today because we reached out for help. What helped us can help you. So don't be afraid to call another recovering addict. *~Narcotics Anonymous Welcome Pamphlet*

'Ike aku, 'ike mai, kokua mai; pela iho la ka nohona 'ohana   (Recognize others, be recognized, help others, be helped; such is a family relationship.) *~Hawaiian Proverb*

Harvest Time

Our Best

Do your best, God does the rest.

Whatever you do in life, do the very best you can with both your heart and mind. ~Lakota Instructions for Living, passed down from White Buffalo Calf Woman (sapphyr.net)

Harvest Time

Learning from All

We never found anyone too dumb to get this program, but we have found some too smart.

Do not let your heart become proud because of what you know; Learn from the ignorant as well as the learned man. ~Ptahhotep, Vizier of Fifth Dynasty King, Isesi, Egypt

Harvest Time

Bough of Hope

Give up control, *but never give up hope.*

If you keep a green bough in your heart,
surely the singing bird will come. ~*Chinese
saying quoted in The Web in the Sea by Alice O.
Howell*

Harvest Time

Road of Time

Today is the first day of the rest of your life.

This is the time that goes forward; it is the road of time, the number of years one is going to live, or the number of times there will be until the end of the world. *~POPOL VUH:, THE MAYAN BOOK OF THE DAWN OF LIFE, Dennis Tedlock*

Harvest Time

Walk the Path of Medicine Way

A spirit of intolerance might repel alcoholics whose lives could have been saved, had it not been for such stupidity. *~Big Book, P 103*

Oh Great Creator, Kiji Manitou, Great One, let me know respect for all things and take responsibility for my own actions as I build my spirit and walk the path of the medicine way. *~Wolfman*

Harvest Time

Be Awake, Be Present

We can reach UP for that energy, and we can reach IN for that energy, feel that life force, touch that Power Greater Than Ourselves. *~Ruth Fishel, Hang in 'Til the Miracle Happens*

"Dreaming" rather than the "Dreamtime" -only because some people act like it is a thing of the past...when it is actually alive and ongoing always and something we live with each day of our lives. *~Marilyn Pittman, Australian Aboriginal Woman*

Harvest Time

The Long Walk

Criticism and finding fault are not spiritual gifts.

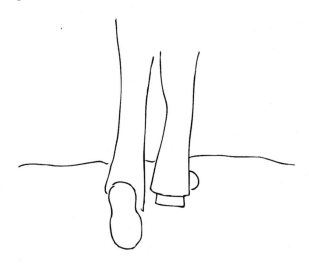

"You mean that you walked all the way over to the ocean and all the way back to give me this shell?" The little Indian boy looked at the teacher and you could kind of see a touch of a tear in his eye. He said, "The long walk is part of the gift!" ~*Native American Indian General Service Office of Alcoholics Anonymous*

Harvest Time

Circle of Service

No one can sincerely try to help another without helping himself." *~Charles Dudley Warner*

Malama Kekahi I kekahi (Take care of each other) *~Hawaiian Proverb*

Harvest Time

Think You Can!

If you think you can or you think you can't,
you're probably right. *~Pocket Sponsor, Day
Seven/4:00 AM*

We are what we think.
All that we are arises with our thoughts.
With our thoughts, we make our world.
~Buddha

Harvest Time

Experience

It takes less time to do something right, than to explain to your sponsor why you did it wrong.

Consult a man of experience,
for he gives you what has cost him much,
and for which you give nothing.
~John Wortabet, [1913], Arabian Wisdom, at
sacred-texts.com

Harvest Time

Get Out of Your Own Way

You can't laugh and think at the same time! So every time you laugh you're getting a break from you. *~Ken D. (P 153, Alkiespeak)*

Let the spirit work in you, without you.
~Unknown

Do not lean too heavily on Reason

Friendly hands had stretched out in welcome.
We were grateful that Reason had brought us
so far. But somehow, we couldn't quite step
ashore. Perhaps we had been leaning too
heavily on Reason that last mile and we did
not like to lose our support. ~*Big Book, P 53*

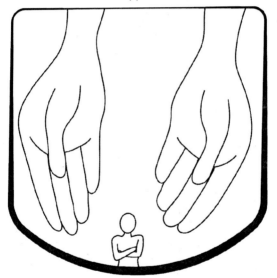

Those who lose dreaming are lost. ~*Australian
Aboriginal Proverb*

Harvest Time

Keep Coming Back

Don't keep coming back. Stay. It works
better that way.

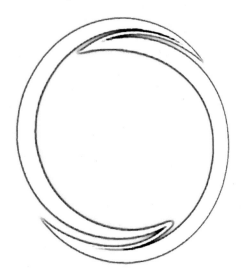

Sharp are the knives against he who
transgresses the road, (he is) without speedy
advance, except when he faults. ~*Instruction
to Kagemni (VIth Dynasty-Papyrus Prisse I & II)*

Harvest Time

Mound of Bones

If you do not pick up up the first fix, pill, or drink--y ou can' t get high, stoned or drunk.

Whiskey is a great and monstrous evil and has reared a high mound of bones. You lose your minds and whiskey causes it all. So now all must say, "I will use it nevermore."
~Handsome Lake, Seneca Nation, around 1800

Harvest Time

Understanding

God, as we understood him...

Once having understood, you should read the teachings of the sages many times." ~*Dogen, The Pocket Zen Reader*

Harvest Time

A Good Life and Beginning

Begin: the rest is easy.

"a good life and beginning": Andres Xiloj commented: "These words would be used in prayer when someone was setting up a new household." ~*Popol Vuh: The Mayan Book of the Dawn of Life,* Copyright 1985, Dennis Tedlock

Harvest Time

Everything on Earth has Purpose

Our primary purpose is to stay free from cocaine and all other mind-altering substances, and to help others achieve the same freedom. *~Cocaine Anonymous*

.... everything on the earth has a purpose, every disease an herb to cure it, and every person a mission. This is the Indian theory of existence. *~Mourning Dove (Salish) 1888-1936*

Harvest Time

Sacred Pathway

Put one foot in front of the other.

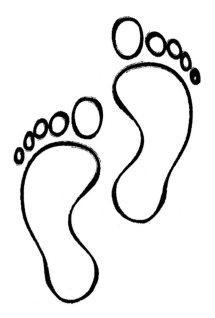

Those who have one foot in the canoe, and one foot in the boat, are going to fall into the river. *~Tuscarora*

Harvest Time

Alcoholic's Anonymous

When anyone anywhere reaches out for help,
I want the hand of AA to be there.

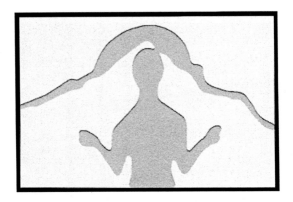

The spiritual philosophy of Alcoholics
Anonymous is parallel to our traditional
Aboriginal beliefs. *Harold, Aboriginal Elder and
Writer*

Harvest Time

In times of Illness

I asked God, 'Why me?' Sometime during my second year in recovery, I began applying the principal of surrender to my illness and developing a closer relationship with my Higher Power. ~*In times of Illness, Narcotics Anonymous*

To me, health is being spiritual, keeping in a good mind. Keeping myself away from the 'evil one', keeping spiritual, keeping strong".
~*Salish Cultural Leader*

Harvest Time

Yawning

What we used to call boredom, we now call serenity.

May I never find myself yawning at life.
~Japanese Christian leader Toyohiko Kagawa
quoted in "Zen and the Art of Anything" by Hal W.
French

12 Step Mission

Don't take service work and the fact that you were chosen lightly. It is a native American theory of existence that we have a mission. It is the Twelve Step theory as well.

...everything on the earth has a purpose, every disease an herb to cure it, and every person a mission. This is the Indian theory of existence. ~*Mourning Dove Salish*

Harvest Time

Expressing Love

Now that we've hit bottom and are starting over clean and sober, we can finally see that without a Higher Power, without love, we are powerless. *~Day By Day, May 4*

Oh Great Spirit, whose voice I hear in the winds and whose breath gives life to everyone, Hear me. I come to you as one of your many children; I am weak, I am small, and need your wisdom, your strength. *~Ojibwa Prayer*

Harvest Time

Stories of the Past

An insiders secret here, some of our best lines have come from AA speaker tapes, especially a lot of lines used by those NA old timers with 14 or more years clean. ~Dalin, NA

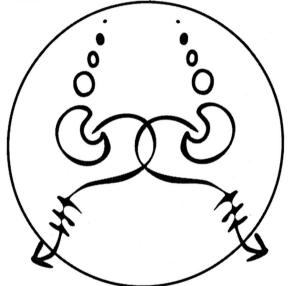

People who spiritually integrate the stories of the past become greatly gifted , while people who disregard the past are doomed to repeat it. ~Seneca Indian Story telling

Harvest Time

Where is God?

Look for your Higher Power everywhere,
because that's where your Higher Power is.
~Walk Softly   and Carry a
Big Book

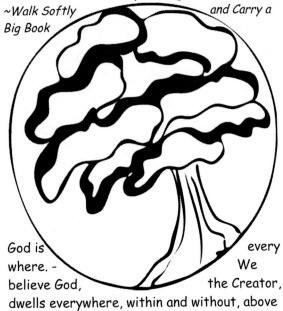

God is   every
where. -   We
believe God,   the Creator,
dwells everywhere, within and without, above
and below. As such, we are bound to respect
all creation, for in that manner we do honor
not only to our Creator, but also to ourselves.
~Statement of Faith from International Aboriginal
Ministries

Harvest Time

When is God?

All in God Time. ~*Walk Softly and Carry a Big Book*

God is "between" the Day and Night. ~*Mayan Daykeepers*

Harvest Time

Who is God?

There are some days when I say: "What program?" "God who?"

To us, Spirit is not a god, goddess or entity of any kind. Spirit is an emanation that defines Creation and gives it a cause, rhyme and rhythm, a reason for being. ~*John Twobirds*

Harvest Time

In the Knowing

The more you have on the inside, the less you need on the outside.

The more you know, the less you need.
~Australian Aboriginal Proverb

Harvest Time

Be Sober

Be sober, be watchful. ~*1 Peter 5, 8*

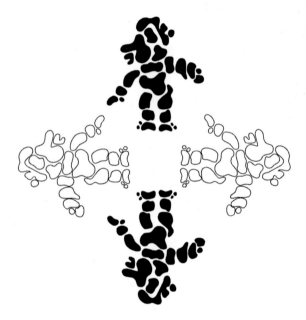

When one prays, as here, asking for things, one looks to heaven; afterwards, when waiting for the blessing, one looks to earth. ~*Andres Xiloj, Mayan Daykeeper*

Harvest Time

When Life Sits Still

It is not so much when things go wrong that we have to watch out for our recovery because we prepare for crisis and are told what to do. It is when things go right that we are caught off guard.

It is the still and silent sea that drowns a man. ~Nordic Saying

Harvest Time

Damage to the Soul

So our troubles, we think, are basically of our own making. They arise out of ourselves, and the alcoholic is an extreme example of self-will run riot, though he usually doesn't think so. ~ *Big Book, p 62*

Other people can rape and damage my body. Only I can damage my soul. ~*American Indian Woman Elder (from Native Wisdom for White Minds)*

Harvest Time

Thoughts are Things

We work at thinking good thoughts, recovery thoughts, sober thoughts. When we sit in the good thoughts, we help make that happen. When we sit in the using thoughts we help make that happen.

One of the first things Seneca children learned was that they might create their own World, their own environment, by visualizing actions and desires in prayer. ~*Twylah Nitcsh, Seneca*

Harvest Time

Silence

"Be still and know that I am God." This can only happen in our silence.

Silence is the absolute poise or balance of body, mind and spirit. ...What are the fruits of silence? They are self-control, true courage or endurance, patience, dignity and reverence. Silence is the cornerstone of character. ~Ohiyesa (1858-1939) a Santee Sioux

Harvest Time

Keeper of the Rituals

Opening the doors to the meeting, making coffee, emptying ashtrays, washing up after and putting away the chairs, these are the rituals that help keep us clean and sober.

Work is regarded as an ennobling virtue. Through work a person gains the respect and admiration of the family and the larger community. ~Cleve Barlow, Maori (from Native Wisdom for White Minds)

Harvest Time

Self-Knowledge

Step 4. Made a searching and fearless moral inventory of ourselves.

Self-mastery is the fruit of self-knowledge.
~Adama Doumbia, Naomi Doumbia, the way of the elders: West African spirituality & tradition

Harmony Restored

We reviewed our own conduct over the years past. Where had we been selfish, dishonest, or inconsiderate? Whom had we hurt? *Big Book, p 69*

In one Navajo healing ceremony, patients sit on a sand painting throughout what is often a four to seven day process to go back through their lives and review them, trying to get from the place of "koyaanisqatsi," where their life went out of balance, to "hozho nahasdlii," to harmony restored.   *~Leslie Gray (Oneida and Seminole ancestry)*

Harvest Time

Open in the Heart

The spiritual principles of Narcotics Anonymous are at the heart of our recovery from the disease of addiction. ~Sponsorship, *"The heart of NA beats when two addicts share their recovery."*

It is said that only when humans are open enough in the heart will there be the deep reconnection that allows a true sharing of the sacred and secret teachings. ~*Ilarion Larry Merculieff is an Aleut (from YES! Magazine)*

Harvest Time

Drunk Alternative

You may be thinking the number one alternative to being drunk is cocaine! heroin! pot! But no, the number one alternative to being drunk is being sober. Don't let the drink take you! ~www.alternativereel.com

Drunk is not Indian.

Harvest Time

Advice

Whenever I ask my sponsor advice about something, she always says, "I don't give advice. Get quiet and ask God. Get on your knees and just talk it over with God."

Is diù nach gabh comhairle, 's diù ghabhas gach comhairle. Who won't take advice is worthless; who takes all advice is the same.
~*Gaelic Indigenousness: Native Gaelic Language Sayings*

Becoming a Sponsor

Becoming a sponsor is like becoming an elder—it is a spiritual transformation, not a chronological progression.

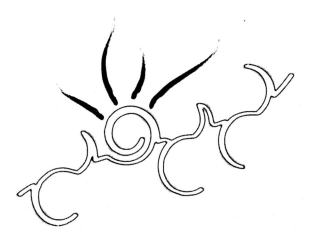

Only God makes one an an elder. Becoming an elder was a spiritual transformation, not chronological progression. Sometimes, the elders would have to tell a man that he was ready, if he was one of those that did not hear God. ~Clyde Grubbs (www.peoplesobold.net)

Harvest Time

Listening is not just Hearing

God gave us one mouth and two ears for a
reason. ~Classic Recovery Saying

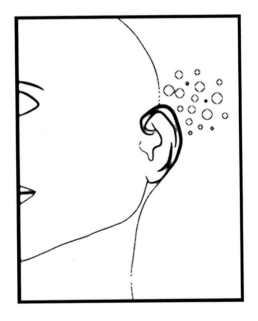

Iti te kupu, nui te korero: Less said speaks
volumes. ~Maori words of wisdom

Harvest Time

HOW (Honest, Openminded, Willing)

Willingness, open-mindedness, and honesty
are vital components of a successful recovery
program. These essential traits are not
something a person can be "convinced" to
possess; they can only come from within.
~Marijuana Anonymous, FAQ www.marijuana-
anonymous.org

The Seneca believed that everything that
made life important came from within.
~Twylah Nitcsh, Seneca

Harvest Time

Advance Daily

One day at a time, remember: The mighty oak
was once a little nut that held its ground.

Throughout your life advance daily, becoming
more skillful than yesterday, tomorrow more
skillful than today. *~Scott Wilson's English
translation of Hagakure, Samurai's Wisdom*

Harvest Time

Waiting for Answers

We are full of questions and we want answers,
answers that just aren't available to us yet.
Our Higher Power will give us the real
answers when we can handle them, not before.
~Day By Day, May 27

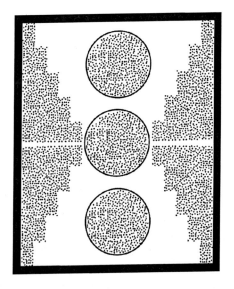

Patience and endurance are of the spirit....
~Joyce Sequichie Hifler, Cherokee Feast of Days

Harvest Time

Rise above Yourself

We remain recovered as long as we remain recovering. We never become drink and drug proof. *~Pocket Sponsor, Day One/6:00 AM*

We are like the tree standing in the middle of a bushfire ... leaves scorched and the bark is ... burnt, but inside, the sap is still flowing and the roots are still strong. Like the tree, we have endured the flames and yet we still have the power to be reborn. *~Miriam Rose Ungunmerr-Baumann, Australian Aboriginal elder*

Harvest Time

Sponsors are Medicine People

A sponsor is a push when stalled, a guide when you're lost, a smile when you're sad—and love.

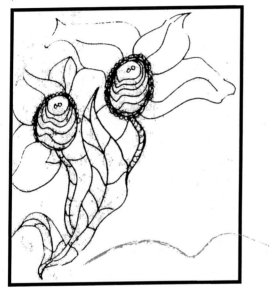

The best gift is that you have allowed for someone to walk their walk in a beautiful way. I honor all medicine people, native, non-native, scientists, educators--all are gifted but should give thanks daily in their heart.
~Uqualla (crossingworlds.com)

Harvest Time

In our Togetherness

We can do together what we could not do alone. We invite you to use our strength and our hope until you have found some of your own. *~Narcotics Anonymous Welcome Pamphlet*

Trí na chéile a thógtar na cáisléain.
In our togetherness (as a team), castles are built. *~Irish Proverbs in Gaelic and English (compassrose.org)*

Harvest Time

Seeing with Compassion

When a person is offended we said to
ourselves, "This is a sick man. How can I be
helpful to him? God save me from being angry.
Thy will be done." ~*Big Book, p 67*

Right View. The right way to think about life
is to see the world through the eyes of the
Buddha--with wisdom and compassion.
~*'Turning of the Dharma Wheel' the Noble
Eightfold Path*

Harvest Time

Free Will

Step Three: Turned our will and our lives over to the care of God, as we understood him.

It is precisely because Man has free will that she is free to break Divine Law and/or frustrate Divine Will... that is, do evil, by definition. God remains submerged in the "unconscious," directing unconscious activities awaiting the person's awakening and developing of the higher divisions of Spirit,
~*The Tree of Life, Kamet, African Cosmology By Grisso*

Harvest Time

From the Promises

That feeling of uselessness and self-pity will disappear. *~Big Book, p. 84*

I cannot think that we are useless or God would not have created us. *~Geronimo*

Harvest Time

We Work Volunteer

Our goal: Not to have something, but to be something. Not to get something, but to give something. Not to rule, but to serve.

We Work Volunteer You could never get people to work this hard if you paid them for it. ~Bruce Stewart, Maori Elder

Harvest Time

Beyond Fear

Trust.

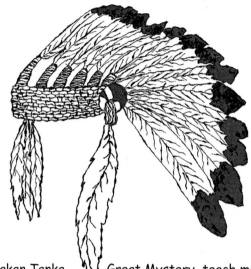

Wakan Tanka, Great Mystery, teach me how to trust my heart, my mind, my intuition, my inner knowing, the senses of my body, the blessings of my spirit. Teach me to trust these things so that I may enter my Sacred Space and love beyond my fear, and thus Walk in Balance with the passing of each glorious Sun. *~Lakota Prayer*

Harvest Time

Dying

Live life today as though you knew you were dying. ~NA Saying

Dying is a process of healing. ~Shea, Toltec Guide

Harvest Time

Winter Solstice

Easy Does It

Don't judge yourself by the way you feel.

Toltec: The Second Agreement

Don't Take Anything Personally. *~Don Miguel Ruiz, Naugle of the Eagle Knight Lineage--Mexico*

Wintertime

Don't forget how you got here

People who spiritually integrate the stories of the past become greatly gifted , while people who disregard the past are doomed to repeat it.

Do not forget the story of remembering.
~Seneca Indian Story telling

Wintertime

Broken Peoples

It doesn't matter what or how much we used.
~NA Basic Text p 19

There are many things to be shared with the
Four Colors of humanity in our common
destiny as one with our Mother the Earth.
*~Resolution of the Fifth Annual Meetings of the
Traditional Elders Circle, 1980*

Wintertime

To Be of Service

Having had a spiritual experience as a result of these Steps we tried to carry this message to others and practice these principles in all our affairs. *~Original version of Step Twelve, Bill Wilson*

To be of service to others, to be of some use to family, community, nation, and the world is one of the main purposes for which human beings have been created. *~Code of Discipline from International Aboriginal Ministries*

Wintertime

Everlasting Truth

There is a principle which is a bar against all information, which is proof against all arguments and which cannot fail to keep a man in everlasting ignorance—that principle is contempt prior to investigation. *~Herbert Spencer*

Three candles dispel the darkness; truth, knowledge and the ways of nature. *~Celtic*

Wintertime

PRIDE

Personal **R**ecovery **I**nvolves **D**efeating the **E**go.

My face is a mask I order to say nothing
About the fragile feelings hiding in my soul
~Glenn Lazore (Mohawk)

Wintertime

Decades Clean

Recently there has been a group for old-timers to get together called "Decades Clean" and it is for ANY Member of Narcotics Anonymous and especially for them that have XX+ years clean so we can find friends from all over the world we have gotten to know over the years.

Make me ever ready to come before you with clean hands and a straight eye,
So as life fades away as a fading sunset,
My spirit may come to you without shame.
~Author Unknown, Ojibwa Prayer

Wintertime

It Works

The program works for those who work it and doesn't for those who don't.

Thus now the salmon run well only for those who work on them carefully." ~Martha Jackson, Ahtna first salmon ritual.

Wintertime

Silent Killer

Alcohol is a silent killer; it destroys little by little until there is nothing left to devour.

Many have fallen with the bottle in their hand. ~*Lakota*

Wintertime

Slotha

We are 12 Step people who practice
Centering Prayer as our 11th Step and pass it
on to others.

"Master, teach us to pray," they asked. Teach
us how to set a trap in which we can catch
God's thoughts and wisdom. *~Aramaic word for
prayer, slotha, means "to set a trap."*

Wintertime

Respect Self

Self-respect is the most important respect you can earn.

Oh great Creator, Kiji Manitou let me be respectful to all: Tecumseh ~*Wisdom of a Shawnee Chief*

Wintertime

Spirit Keepers

Are not some of us just as biased and unreasonable about the realm of the spirit as were the ancients about the realm of the material? ~*AA Big Book, P 51*

...Spirit Keepers are the true warriors of today. In diminishing pockets throughout the world, in many ways disrespected, they still maintain the invisible threads that connect us to our roots. ~*Kenosis Spirit Keepers*

Wintertime

Speaking Truth with Kindness

To the desolate alcoholic, the act of kindness can be the difference.

God choose you, to show the way –
May we love the country, as you did,
May we speak the truth with kindness, May
we love the family and all our people, as you
did. ~Marilynn P., Koori Tribe of Aboriginal
Australia

Wintertime

Voice of the Great Spirit

God speaks to us in many ways at many times.
If we are spiritually alert, we will know it
when it happens. A stray thought occurs; we
overhear a bit of conversation, a passage in
something we are reading suddenly stands out
—and we know we have connected. *~In God's
Care, March 13*

The voice of the Great Spirit is heard in the
twittering of birds, the rippling of mighty
waters, and the sweet breathing of flowers.
~Zitkala-Sa (Dakota Sioux)

Wintertime

Knowing What to Do

This time, like all times, is a very good one if we but know what to do with it. *~Ralph Waldo Emerson.*

Those who think they can, will accomplish something. *~Iñupiat People, Eskimos of Alaska*

Wintertime

Warrior Song

This painful past may be of infinite value to other families still struggling with their problem. *~The Big Book, The Family Afterward, P 124*

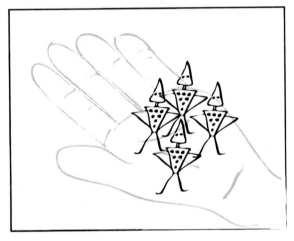

There's an ancient 'Warrior Song' that says, 'There is meaning only in the struggle. Triumph or defeat is in the hands of God. So let us continue the struggle.' *~Linda Tippett, a staff writer for Mature Living Magazine. Internet article, The Invisible Cloak*

Wintertime

Books of our Program

What I know today is that much of what I initially found so amazingly profound from the long-timers when I came in can be found in the books of our program. ~*Walk Softly & Carry a Big Book*

O ka makapo
mea hapapa i
Only the blind
darkness. ~*Hawaiian Proverb*

wale no ka
ka pouli:
grope in the

Wintertime

Pain and Spiritual Tools

You might expect too much of yourself.
"Take it like a man," you may think. Why don't
you relax and try "taking it like a child?" How
would a child take it? Openly and honestly.

Great Spirit, today, give me the tools to seek
peace of mind. ~*Spirited Wolf*

Wintertime

Visions of the Night

In a dream, in a vision of the night, when deep sleep falleth upon men, in slumberings upon the bed; then He openeth the ears of men, and sealeth their instruction." ~*Job 33, 14-16.*

All dreams spin out from the same web. ~*Hopi Saying*

Wintertime

Setting a Trap for God

When they talked of a God personal to me, Who was love, superhuman strength and direction, I became irritated and my mind snapped shut against such a theory. ~*AA Big Book, p 10*

We can trap all the love, joy, truth, peace, energy, and compassion we need when we are receptive to all which is rightly ours. It's truly an attitude of heart and mind that prepares us for whatever is necessary. ~*Setting a Trap for God, The Aramaic Prayer of Jesus*, by Rocco A. Errico

Wintertime

Cleanse Yourself

Step 9: Made direct amends to such people wherever possible, except when to do so would injure them or others.

Cleanse yourself before your own eyes, lest another cleanse you. ~*The Instruction of Hordedef (Vth Dynasty) Egyptian*

Wintertime

Song of Birds

Learn to listen. Opportunity sometimes knocks very softly.

Oh Great Spirit, teach me to think quietly, to speak gently, and to hear Thy voice in the whispering breeze, the song of birds and in the murmuring brook. ~*A Native American Prayer (Cherokee)*

Wintertime

Slippery Places

Those that hang in slippery places, slip.

Those that lie down with dogs, get up with fleas. *~Blackfoot*

Wintertime

Live Yourself Sober

You cannot think yourself sober, read
yourself sober or act yourself sober. You
must live yourself sober.

Right Conduct. No matter what we say, others
know us from the way we behave. Before we
criticize others, we should first see what we
do ourselves. ~ *'Turning of the Dharma Wheel'
the Noble Eightfold Path*

Wintertime

Practice these Principles

We practice these principles in all our affairs.
The principles are found in Steps one through
twelve.

Three things must be united before good can
come of them; thinking well, speaking well, and
acting well. ~*Ancient Celtic*

Wintertime

My Will, My Life

God, Take my Will and my life, guide me in my recovery and show me how to live ... CLEAN!
~NA 3rd Step Prayer

Lead me, O God, and thou, O Destiny! as well as these. If this be God's will, so let it be!
~Golden Sayings, Epictetus, Greek

Wintertime

Don't Try

Don't ever *try* to stop drinking. Stop drinking.

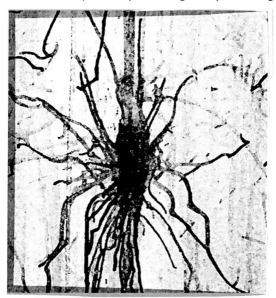

All the Buddhas of all the ages have been telling you a very simple fact: Be - don't try to become. Within these two words, be and becoming, your whole life is contained. Being is enlightenment, becoming is ignorance.
~Buddha

Wintertime

Asking for Help

Being addicted is like being trapped in a box, and the instructions for getting out of the box are on the outside. You need someone to read them to you. But you have to ask.

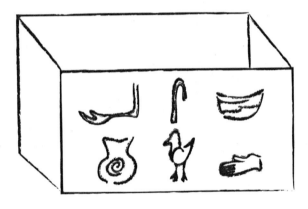

Do you want to know who is a real Medicine Man? He is the one who doesn't say, "I am a Medicine Man." He doesn't ask you to come to him. You have got to go and ask him. And you will always find he is there amongst his own people. *~Louis Farmer, Onondaga (from Native Wisdom for White Minds)*

Wintertime

Done or Undone

Step 9. Made direct amends to such people wherever possible except when to do so would injure them or others.

Pay no attention to the faults of others, things done or left undone by others. Consider only what by oneself is done or left undone. *~Buddha*

Wintertime

How to Pray & Meditate

It is to be hoped that every A.A. {...} will return to the practice of {meditation} as never before. But what about the rest of us who, less fortunate, don't even know how to begin? *~12 & 12, p 98 – 102*

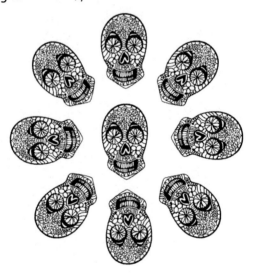

It takes nine years to learn how to pray.
~Huichol Teaching of Sierra Madre Mountains, Western Mexico

Wintertime

Healing & Humble

Humility is being a part of the whole, not apart from the whole. ~*Walk Softly and Carry a Big Book*

Healing will continue in a right path as long as we are honoring and humble, things come automatically. It harmonizes with our capabilities. People stimulate a part of you that will allow for healing to continue, to touch heart places. ~*Uquallan (crossingworlds.com)*

Wintertime

Use not because of Days Past

There is nothing so bad that a drink or a drug
won't make it worse. ~*A Sponsor's Adage*

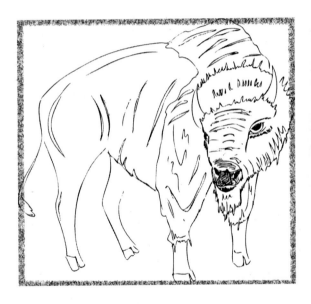

Without freedom from the past there is no
freedom at all... ~*J. Krishnamurti, The Book of
Life*

Wintertime

Unity in Recovery

One Disease, One Program. ~*Narcotics Anonymous Slogan*

Pupukahi i holomua. (Unite in order to progress.) ~*Hawaiian Proverb*

Wintertime

Why shouldn't we laugh?

Outsiders are sometimes shocked when we burst into merriment over a seemingly tragic experience out of the past. But why shouldn't we laugh? We have recovered, and have been given the power to help others. *~AA Big Book, p 132*

Humor is the WD-40 of healing. *~George Goddstriker, Kainai (Blackfoot) Elder, Canada from Native Wisdom for White Minds)*

Wintertime

Kindness

If there is someone weaker than you, be kind to them. If there is someone stronger than you, be kind to yourself. *~Walk Softly and Carry a Big Book*

Whether one believes in a religion or not, and whether one believes in rebirth or not, there isn't anyone who doesn't appreciate kindness and compassion. *~Dalai Lama*

Wintertime

Correction

The man who makes a mistake and doesn't correct it, makes two.

Everyone needs to be corrected sometime, even when they are right. ~*Maori Elder*

Wintertime

Involve Me

As someone said: "You can probably get clean by just coming to meetings. However, if you want to stay clean and experience recovery, you will need to practice the Twelve Steps." ~*Narcotics Anonymous Welcome Pamphlet*

Tell me and I'll forget. Show me, and I may not remember. Involve me, and I'll understand. ~*Tribe Unknown*

Wintertime

Right Effort

If I had only been willing to change my lifestyle, I could have had a life worth living so much sooner. *~CDA First Edition, P 362*

6. Right Effort. A worthwhile life means doing our best at all times and having good will toward others. This also means not wasting effort on things that harm ourselves and others. *~'Turning of the Dharma Wheel' the Noble Eightfold Path*

Wintertime

How do we want to be treated?

When was the last time we vented our frustration on a sales clerk, even though we wouldn't want them to do that to us?
~Conscious Contact, Sept 6

Be grateful, One to Another, and Have Love for one another....I think a Pretty neat Jewish Fellow said that two thousand years ago, they are good words to follow. ~Mitakuye Oyasin
www.terramaterint.org

Wintertime

The Easier Way

It is 2.5 times easier to smile than to frown.
It takes 43 muscles to frown, but only 17 to
smile. *~Karlynn Baker Scharlau*

You mean, everyone isn't as happy as we are?
*~Tsering Dolma, Ladakhi Farmer (from Native
Wisdom for White Minds)*

Wintertime

Circle Teachings

Our program does not teach us how to handle drinking and drugging. It teaches us how to handle recovery.

But time and again our Elders have said that the 12 Steps of AA

are just the same as the principles that our ancestors lived by, with only one change. When we place the 12 Steps in a circle then they come into alignment with the circle teachings that we know from many of our tribal ways. ~Red Road, P 48

Wintertime

Big Shadow

Worry gives a small thing a big shadow.

Turn your face to the sun and the shadows fall behind you. *~Maori Proverb—New Zealand*

Wintertime

Look to this Day

This is a daily program. It can only be done one day at a time.

Look to this day
This very life of life
In its brief course lie all
The realities and verities of existence
  ~Sanskrit Prayer

Wintertime

Time for Dreams

Take time to dream, it is what the future is made of. *~Eccl. 3:1*

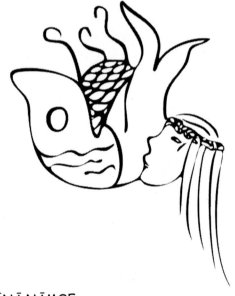

NĀNĀ NĀMOE.
> Look to your dreams. *~Hawaiiana*

Wintertime

Center of the World

Selfishness - self-centeredness! That, we
think, is the root of our troubles. ~*Big book, p
62*

But anywhere is the center of the world.
~*Black Elk , Holy Man of the Oglala Sioux*

Wintertime

There is never a single footprint

There are only two things an alcoholic doesn't
like: the way things are, and change.

One foot may lead us to an evil way, the other
foot may lead us to a good. So are all things
two, all two. *~Eagle Chief (Letakos-Lesa) Pawnee*

Wintertime

Strong Kinship

Joining a 12 Step program is like coming home and finding your long lost family.

See connections. All things are related.
~Walkie Charles, Yup'ik People, Eskimos of South West Alaska

Wintertime

Speak Honorably

Don't just talk the talk.

Isn't your speech good, and your walk? ~*Popol vuh:, the Mayan Book of the Dawn of Life, Dennis Tedlock*

Wintertime

The Real Power

My own experience has been that, the more
the old timers learn what early A.A. was really
like, the more they want to know; and the
more they tend to return to the precepts of
the original Akron A.A. *~The Real Power Behind
Alcoholic's Anonymous*

Living here in my Grandmothers Country is
changing me in so many ways. I feel a lot more
connected to this as a sober person. Living
here in the bush I feel the presence of the
land much more strongly. *~Kiola Beach, Australia*

Wintertime

Room for All

There is room in MA for all beliefs. *~Marijuana Anonymous' book Life With Hope, p 7*

The Great Spirit is our Father, but the Earth is our Mother. She nourishes us; that which we put into the ground, She returns to us.... *~Big Thunder (Bedagi), late 19th century Algonquin*

Wintertime

The Ground is our Home

The body-soul is a citizen of that realm we call heaven, as much as the body-physical is a citizen of the land we call home. ~Edgar Cayce, Reading 2823-1

I wonder if the ground has anything to say? I wonder if the ground is listening to what is said? {...}The ground says, it is the great spirit that placed me here. ~Young Chief, 1855 Treaty Council

Wintertime

Dig a Hole for Grief

It isn't destructive to feel sorry for ourselves; it's destructive to stay stuck feeling sorry for ourselves.

Go out into the woods. Dig a hole in the ground near a tree or bush. Pour all of your feelings into that hole. When you are finished, cover the hole. Thank the tree (or bush) for listening and witnessing your grief process. Thank Mother Earth for receiving your grief. ~*Journey of Hearts: A Healing Place in CyberSpace, "Ways of Coping"*

Wintertime

What is life?

Life involves the interplay of black and white. In other words, the gray area is where life takes place. A big part of the healing process is learning {and...} recognizing that life is not black and white. *~Codependence: The Dance of Wounded Souls*

What is life? It is the flash of a firefly in the night. It is the breath of a buffalo in the wintertime. It is the little shadow which runs across the grass and loses itself in the sunset.
   ~Blackfoot

Wintertime

Do Not Fight Among Yourselves

Conflict cannot survive without our participation and when we work on ours, theirs have a wonderful way of disappearing because we don't participate! *~Conscious Contact, Dec 13*

No tree has branches so foolish as to fight among themselves. *~Native American Saying*

Wintertime

To Know Something

No chart, graph, or stack of pamphlets and books can convince someone that they have a problem if they themselves are unwilling to admit it. *~Marijuana Anonymous, FAQ*
www.marijuana-anonymous.org

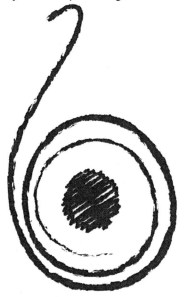

To know something we must become one with it. *~Spirited Wolf*

Wintertime

Oral Tradition

The Sleeping Beauty story is the best story
to use in these Steps, but in other teaching
stories like Beauty and the Beast, there is
the same principle
employed, that of
facing fear and
distaste and the
change that is
granted.
~*Change
With the
Twelve
Steps*

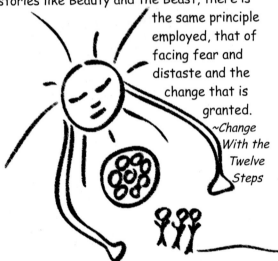

I ask that you look at these teachings as a
way for these folks of no known Native blood,
to find a way to live with this Good Mother
Earth, as well as with all her Children in
peace, balance, and Beauty. ~*Mitakuye Oyasin*
www.terramaterint.org

Wintertime

Do Right

Do the right thing, not the self-righteous thing. *~12-Step program advice from a sponsor*

No one is hurt by doing the right thing.
~Hawaiian Proverb

Wintertime

Our Friends Make Us Human

Some of us become afraid that we are using our friends like we did in our old drugging days. The difference today is that we are using a *friend*, and we expect them to use us as well. ~*Conscious Contact, April 11*

Caring is the practice of concern and oneness. It is putting the problems, interests and circumstances of others at a higher level of attention. We are human through our interaction with others. Without others we are not human. ~*Pillar of Ubuntu Living*

Wintertime

Space in Between

There's God's will and there's your will and there's a space in between. If you do the work, eventually the space will disappear and it will be God's will. ~*Walk Softly and Carry a Big Book*

Neither I, nor anything I attempt to do, will work without our Creator. Being Indian and being spiritual has the same meaning. Spirituality is our gift from the Great One. This day, I vow to walk the Red Road. ~*whitebison.org*

Wintertime

More Drink, Less Knowing

Today I am leading a life. When drinking, I was a life being led. ~*Speaker at a meeting*

Less good than they say for the sons of men is the drinking oft of ale: for the more they drink, the less they know about the nature of men. ~*Hávamál, st. 12 (Nordic)*

Wintertime

Letting Go

We always have the option of continuing to hold on but change will still happen. It is when the pain of holding on becomes greater than the fear of letting go that we finally let go. ~Conscious Contact, Aug 25

When you discover you are riding a dead horse, the best strategy is to dismount. ~Dakota Tribal Saying

Wintertime

Begin Where You Are

Don't let your starting point in recovery ever discourage you. Anyone who gets to be an Old Timer had to begin where they were.

Don't take another mouthful before you have swallowed what is in your mouth. ~*Madagascar Wisdom*

Wintertime

Road to Recovery

When you think of yesterday without regret
and tomorrow without fear, you are on the
road to recovery.

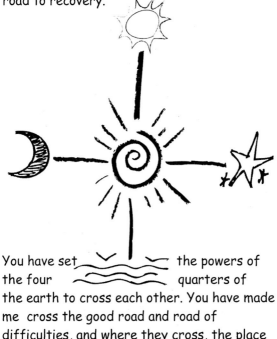

You have set the powers of
the four quarters of
the earth to cross each other. You have made
me cross the good road and road of
difficulties, and where they cross, the place
is holy. *~Black Elk: Holy Man of the Oglala Sioux
1863-1950*

Wintertime

Medicine People

A sponsor by any other name is still a sponsor.

Medicine people, shamans, healers have many names. There are many spirits such as rock spirits, tree spirits. Humans each are given giftings to facilitate a particular medicine. All are unique." ~Uqualla (crossingworlds.com)

Wintertime

Knowing Needs

Success is not getting what you want; it's knowing what you don't need.

The more you know, the less you need.
~*Australian Aboriginal Proverb*

Wintertime

Balance

Turning our lives around means we are striving for balance. ~*Conscious Contact, September 20*

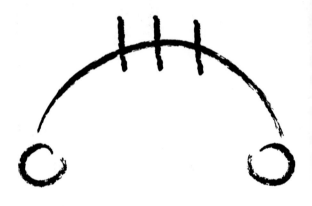

Cha'n fhiach bròn a ghnàth, 'S cha'n fhiach ceòl a ghnàth. Sorrowing always is not good, And music (mirth) always is not good. ~*Gaelic Indigenousness: Native Gaelic Language Sayings*

Wintertime

Remaking Yourself

No one can work your program for you, not your parents, not your sponsor, not your spiritual leader. Only you can do this.

As human beings, our greatness lays not so much in being able to remake the world... as in being able to remake ourselves, *~Mahatma Gandhi*

Wintertime

Setting his Mind to Work

You have to drink alcohol in order to get drunk. You have to work the program in order for it to work. *~Pocket Sponsor, Day Thirteen/4:00 PM*

One should search throughout his whole life how best to follow the Way. And he should study, setting his mind to work without putting things off. Within this is the Way. *~Scott Wilson's English translation of Hagakure, Samurai's Wisdom*

Wintertime

Hot Pot of Stubbornness

Our own stubbornness will either lead us to a break down or a break through. If we are doing Step Eleven, chances are, we'll have the break through.

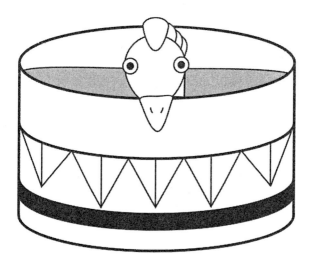

A stubborn chicken learns its lesson in a hot pot of soup. ~African Tribal

Great Forgiving

Forgiveness detoxifies. *~Walk Softly and Carry a Big Book*

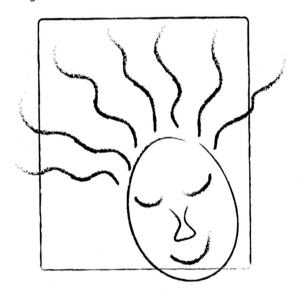

And we need a Great Forgiving, ...But healing can't begin without Forgiveness. We must Forgive each other, our loved ones, our friends, our enemies, ourselves. *~Chief Arvol Looking Horse: Prayer for Peace, Healing and Forgiveness*

Wintertime

Spring Equinox

Honesty

...a manner of living which demands rigorous honesty. Big Book, p 58

Toltec: The First Agreement

Be Impeccable with Your Word *~Don Miguel Ruiz, Naugle of the Eagle Knight Lineage--Mexico*

Springtime

Choose Your Own

My friend suggested what then seemed a novel idea. He said, "Why don't you choose your own conception of God?" *~Big Book, P 12*

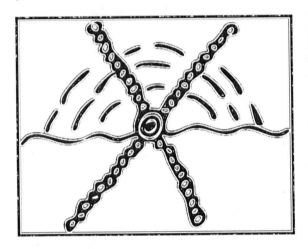

Creation, the Mystery--in Algonquin, the root language of Tsalagi, it is Ywahoo, the "Great Mystery," beyond the form of words. There is no word for "God"; we call it a great Mystery, because of its formlessness. *~Dhyani Ywahoo, Voices of our Ancestors-Cherokee Teachings*

Springtime

Givers & Takers

Our spiritual recovery remains dependent on this principle: gaining the balance between giving and taking. *~Conscious Contact, Nov 3rd*

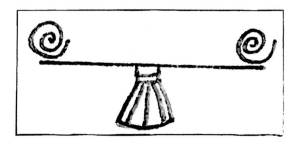

Of giving and receiving. Just like breathing, we must exhale in order to inhale. Life and nature operate on reciprocity. There is a fair exchange of energy. It is about balanced flow. *~Hirini Reedy, NgatiPorou tribe of Maori (interview from lostartsofthemind.com)*

Springtime

Change in Self

A change has taken place, one so fundamental
that it will not yield to pain, doubt, or denial.
Whether one likes it or not, the change in
self is here to stay.
~CDA First Edition., P 79

Can we change our focus,
With no need to defend?
Acknowledging joy and sorrow,
Without judging foe or friend? *~Jamie Sams,
The Promise of Tomorrow*

Springtime

How tough is the ground?

Qualifications for me to help you, 1) you have to need it, 2) you have to want it, 3) you have to ask for it, 4) you have to ask *me*. ~*An Old-Timer*

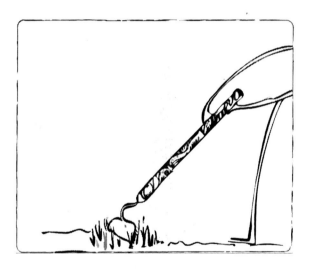

If the new hoe wishes to know how tough the ground is, let him ask the old hoe. ~*Jamaican*

Springtime

Waking the Brain

They tell us that even if our ass falls off, we should put it in a bag and take it to a meeting. There's a reason for that because there's a good chance your brain is in the bag too.
~Jumpin' Joe

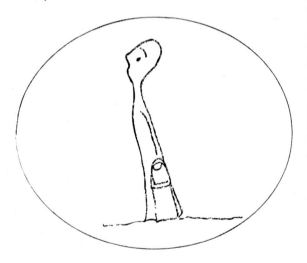

You can't wake a person who is pretending to be asleep. ~Navajo Wisdom

Springtime

Aloha

Living in Fellowship: Perhaps nothing else exists that can so completely multiply all our joys and divide all our grief. *~Day By Day*

Aloha is the unconditional desire to promote the true good of other people in a friendly spirit out of a sense of kinship. *~Abraham Akaka, Hawaiian Elder*

Springtime

Be Here We Are

I pray for the willingness to be willing to be willing to let go absolutely. *~Meeting Wisdom, P 97*

May as well be here we are as where we are. *~Australian Aboriginal Proverb*

Springtime

Creator's Way

Religion is man talking to man about God.
Spirituality is God and Man talking.

Many churches and religions try to teach
morality and create laws and rules to control
what Creator made naturally. If we learn and
practice respect for all things, morality will
follow, that is the natural way, Creators way.

Springtime

Talking Circles

The morning after my first meeting I woke up and heard the birds singing and knew it was the birds.

We bring our addicted brothers and sisters to the fish camps deep in the wild. We detox in the sweat lodge and then sit in talking circles around the camp fire and tell our stories. That is our meeting. *~Athabaskan Elder, sober 30 years*

Springtime

Drink Takes You

First you take a drink, then the drink takes a drink, then the drink takes you. *~F. Scott Fitzgerald*

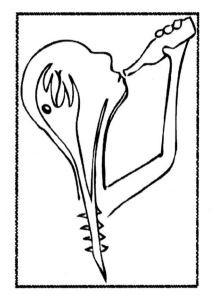

Ged b'e gheibheadh a roghainn, 's mairg a thaghadh an diù. Pity him who has his choice, and chooses the worse. *~Native Gaelic Language Sayings*

Springtime

Stillness

Don't be impatient with the universe—it sure hasn't been impatient with you!

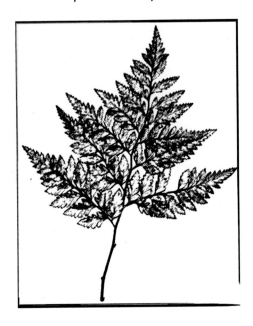

When you are in doubt, be still, and wait; when doubt no longer exists for you, then go forward with courage. *~Ponca Chief White Eagle*

Springtime

Teachings of the Sages

The AA Big Book, the NA Basic Text, the CDA First Edition and White Bison's Red Road do not need to be rewritten; they need to be reread.

He who would do great things should not attempt them all alone. -*Seneca*

Springtime

Working Works

Members of CDA have learned that if you work the steps, they *will* work. The only time they do not work is when you do not work them. *~Conscious Contact, Jan 5*

If you do not gather firewood you cannot keep warm. *~Angola, Namibia- Ovambo*

Springtime

Expect Miracles

If you can't expect a miracle, at least expect a coincidence.

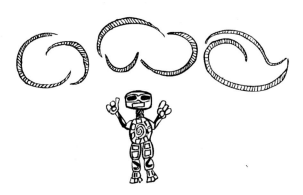

Whaia te iti kahuranga ki te tuahu koe me he maunga teitei: Aim for the highest cloud so that if you miss it, you will hit a lofty mountain. ~*Maori Proverb*

Springtime

Medicine Within

Faith was the first medicine known to man.
~*Walk Softly and Carry a Big Book*

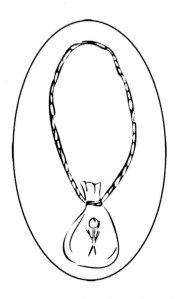

"Medicine" in Native thought means "sacred",
"power", "healing"-- that is as near as I can
explain in words what I understand in heart,
mind and spirit. Each Being has his/her own
"Medicine" ~*Star Spider Dancing*

Springtime

Lucky Day

Any failure will tell you—success is nothing but luck. ~*Walk Softly and Carry a Big Book*

Fools wait for a lucky day but every day is a lucky day for an industrious man. ~*Buddha*

Springtime

Admitting Mistakes

Step 10. Continued to take personal inventory and when we were wrong promptly admitted it.

A ua sala uta, ia tonu tai: When a mistake has been made inland, it should be rectified at the seaside. ~Samoan Proverb, samoalive.com

Springtime

Yesterday is Ashes

Yesterday is history, tomorrow a mystery,
but today is a gift, that's why we call it the
'Present." *~Popular Recovery Slogan*

Yesterday wood; tomorrow is ashes. Only
today the fire shines brightly. *~Eskimo Proverb*

Springtime

A Duck is a Duck is a Duck

If it walks like a duck and it waddles like a duck and it quacks like a duck, then it must be a duck.

When all men say you are a dog, it is time to bark. ~Africana, Togo

Springtime

Way of Life

The 12 Step Programs are not religious; they are a spiritual way of life.

Our ancestors did not have a religion, they had a Way of Life. ~*Star Spider Dancing*

Springtime

Forgive Before One Offends

Forgive yourself because your Spiritual
Source already has. Who are you to argue?
~Pocket Sponsor, Day Eight/4:00 PM

When visiting another village in Fiji, the Chief
will sit you down, take your offering and then
forgive you for whatever you may do to
offend. You are forgiven your shortcomings
before they manifest. *~Fijian Way of Life*

Springtime

Accepting the Sorrows

Gratitude and acceptance always help, no matter what the circumstances.

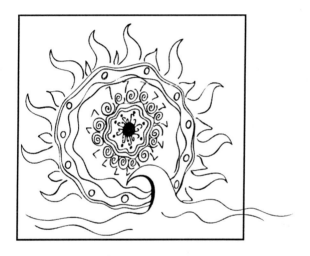

Thank you creator for the blessing of understanding and accepting the valleys of sorrows and memories that still dwell within the bones and the smiles and the blood of our grandfathers and grandchildren. *~Love Walela*

Springtime

Prayers with Feet

Prayers that are answered are Prayers with feet.

In prayer, then, we are adjusting and preparing our minds and hearts to receive God's program. ~*Rocco A. Errico, Setting a Trap for God, The Aramaic Prayer of Jesus*

Springtime

Resistance

If you resist it, it gets worse; if you accept it, it gets better.

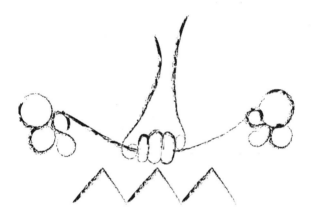

Force, no matter how concealed, begets resistance. ~*Lakota*

Springtime

Become Desperate

Bottom: No one comes to a 12 Step program on a good day.

The Way of the Samurai is in desperateness. Ten men or more cannot kill such a man. Common sense will not accomplish great things. Simply become insane and desperate. *~Scott Wilson's English translation of Hagakure, Samurai's Wisdom*

Springtime

Circle of Recovery

It is suggested that recovery begins when you have learned enough from those before you and pass it along to those behind. Love is the process that keeps the circle moving.
~Pocket Sponsor,
Day Twenty-
five/4:00 AM

The life of a man
is a circle from
childhood to childhood, and so it is in
everything where power moves. *~Black Elk,*
Holy Man of the Oglala Sioux

Springtime

Balance

If we look closely, we will see we are given even amounts of blessings and sorrows.

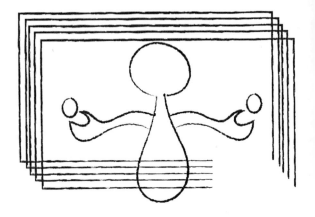

Cha'n fhiach bròn a ghnàth, 'S cha'n fhiach ceòl a ghnàth. Sorrowing always is not good, And music always is not good. ~*Gaelic*

Springtime

Pure Gift of Gratitude

We grow in gratitude for the pure gift of being clean and sober. In time we recognize and are grateful for its benefits. *~Day By Day, February 24*

Are we learning to show gratitude, For the victories over human pain? *~Jamie Sams, The Promise of Tomorrow*

Springtime

Let Go or Do Not Let Go

I pray for the willingness to be willing to be
willing to let go absolutely. *~Meeting Wisdom,
P 97*

Go--or do not go--to the god your Lord.
~Sumerian Proverb (4000-2000 BC)

Springtime

Negative Warriors

This is a Positive Program for Negative people.

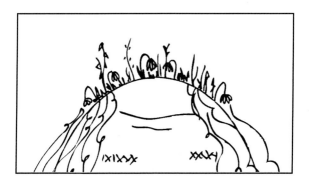

As negative warriors we tend to be attackers, fault finders and judgmental people. We feel guilty and will use words of guilt to shame other people. {...} If you recognize yourself in this description, it might mean you have the honesty to work these Steps. *~Red Road, P 57*

Springtime

Positive Warriors

Fill your head with positive thoughts and there won't be room for the negative.

Positive warriors are grounded in the love-based thought system. {...} They feel a great deal of unity, harmony, and balance in their lives. ~Red Road, P 57

Springtime

Consequences

Insanity is doing the same thing over and over again and expecting different results.

He who considers consequences will attain his object, and he who does not carefully think on them, evil will be sure to overtake him. ~*John Wortabet, [1913], Arabian Wisdom, at sacred-texts.com*

Springtime

Do not pick up the Clump of Clay

You're powerless over the first drink, but not powerless over your choices. ~*Walk Softly and Carry a Big Book*

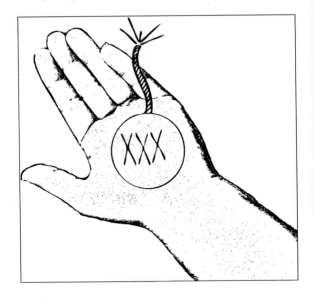

Would you place a lump of clay in the hand of him who throws? ~*Sumerian Proverb*

Springtime

Give Thanks for Life Within

Gratitude makes sense of our past, brings peace for today, and creates a vision for tomorrow. ~Melody Beattie

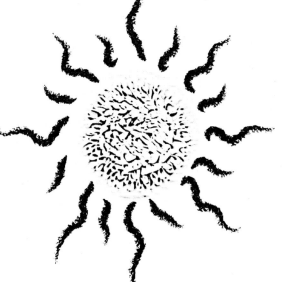

Each morning upon arising and each evening before sleeping, give thanks for the life within you and for all life. ~Sacred Earth New

Springtime

Small Steps

Don't let your starting point in recovery ever discourage you. Don't let your starting point today put a frown on your face. Anyone who gets to be an old-timer had to be a newcomer first. *~Pocket Sponsor, Day Ten/3:00 PM*

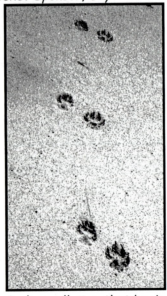

It is the single small step that begins the journey of a thousand miles. *~Lao-Tzo, A Path and A Practice, Chapter 64*

Springtime

Listen when Creator Speaks

God speaks through people, don't worry about which ones.

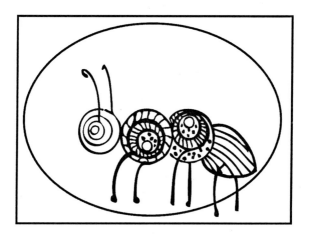

One should pay attention to even the smallest crawling creatures, for these, too, may have a valuable lesson to teach us, and even the smallest ant may wish to communicate with a person. *-Black Elk, Holy Man of the Oglala Sioux*

Springtime

Difficult to Carry

It's not when things are going badly that we are in the most danger; it's when things are going really well.

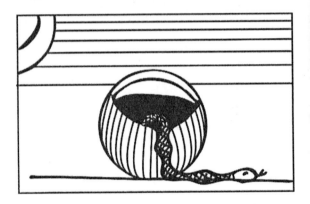

An uair as laine 'n cupan, 's ann as dorr' a ghiulan. When the cup is fullest it is most difficult to carry. ~*Native Gaelic Language Sayings*

Two Choices

This is a program of suggestions. For 'suggestion' you have two choices: Take it or leave it. *~What a sponsor may say to his sponsee*

A good soldier is a poor scout. *~Cheyenne*

Springtime

When One Errors

Some of us learn by other people's mistakes;
the rest of us have to be the other people.
*~Anonymous, How to Become an Old-timer, Don't
Drink and Don't Die*

When two persons are engaged in an
undertaking and one makes an error, the
other can still save the situation by setting
things right again. *~Samoan Proverb*

Springtime

Intelligence in Recovery

Two things alcoholics and addicts have in common: We are all chemically dependent, and we all think we're smarter than everyone else.

There is a saying: intelligence is like hairs -- everybody has her or his own. ~*Haya Proverb in Tanzania*

Springtime

Key to Survival

We've learned in NA that we can apply spiritual principles to help us get through these difficult times. When we admit that we are powerless, we can accept our illness and any necessary medical treatment. ~*Mark E, Toronto*

Conciliation is the key to survival. Peace is the goal. ~*Haida Gwaii, Traditional Circle of Elders*

Springtime

The Best Healer

Although its simple, it is not easy to get clean and sober. In fact, this will be the hardest thing you have ever done.

A'chungaidh leighis is goirte,
Si is moth'tha deaneamh feum.
The medicine (or liniment) that hurts the most Is generally the best healer. ~*Gaelic Indigenousness: Native Gaelic Language Sayings*

Springtime

Incorrect thoughts are not You

Don't romance the drink. Don't romance the
drug. Don't romance the high.

Those thoughts you feel are incorrect, let
them go. They are not you. What is truly you
is ever beautiful and ever in the stream.
*~Dhyani Ywahoo, Voices of our Ancestors-
Cherokee Teachings*

Springtime

Words Exiting your Mouth

When you talk, you can only say something you already know. When you listen, you may learn something somebody else knows.

Pa`a ka waha: Observe, be silent and learn.
~*Hawaiian Proverb*

Springtime

Accept

Acceptance was his key to liberation. ~*Doctor, Alcoholic, Addict, AA Big Book*

Accept what life brings. You cannot control many things. ~*Philip Kelly, Aleut People, Aleutians*

Springtime

Sweat Lodge

Step 6. We were entirely ready to have God remove all these defects of character.

The sweat lodge is also a good place to say, "We were entirely ready to have God remove all these defects of character," and, "to humbly ask him to remove our shortcomings."
~Lakota Elder, The Red Road to Wellbriety. P 7

Springtime

Brotherhood

Do not put the "sole purpose" of any
fellowship above the "soul purpose."

Out of the Indian   approach to life
there came a great   freedom, an
intense and absorbing   respect for life,
enriching faith in a   Supreme Power,
and principles of truth, honesty, generosity,
equity, and brotherhood as a guide to
mundane relations. -Black Elk, Holy Man of the
Oglala Sioux

Springtime

From Inside

They say it's an inside job.

I ask my Higher Power to be within and about
me. *~Rod Betonney, Navajo*

Springtime

Create the Healing

Every thought you have can be part of a continuous prayer and everything you do can be your practice of healing. *~Pocket Sponsor Day 1, 10 am*

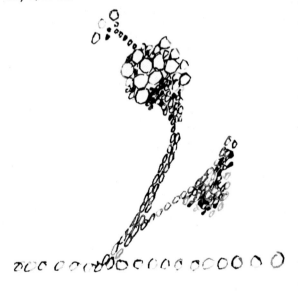

You will need to create your own reality, one in which you can do your healing. *~Shaman from "New Mexico", C. Rowa*

Springtime

The Ground Says

Every blade of grass has its angel that bends
over it and whispers, "Grow, grow." ~*Tulmud*

The ground
says, the
great spirit
has placed
me here to
produce all
that grows
on me, trees and fruit. The great spirit, in
placing men on the earth, desired them to
take good care of the ground and to do each
other no harm. ~*Young Chief, 1855 Treaty
Council*

Springtime

Speak Straight

Absolute Honesty: Both with ourselves and with others, in word, deed, and thought.
~First of the Four Absolutes of the Oxford Movement

You must speak straight so that your words may go as sunlight into our hearts. *~Cochise "Hardwood" 1874*

Springtime

Unselfish

Absolute Unselfishness: To be willing
wherever possible to help others in need.
~Second of the Four Absolutes of the Oxford
Movement

My Religion is simple; My Religion is kindness.
~Dalai Lama

Springtime

Straight from the Heart

Absolute Love: To love God with our whole heart, mind, and soul, and to love our neighbors as ourselves. ~*Third of the Four Absolutes of the Oxford Movement*

Our first teacher is our own heart. ~*Cheyenne*

Springtime

Right Mindfulness

Absolute Purity: Integrity and clarity of mind, of body, and of purpose. ~*Fourth of the Four Absolutes of the Oxford Movement*

Right Mindfulness. This means being aware of our thoughts, words, and deeds. ~*'Turning of the Dharma Wheel' the Noble Eightfold Path, Number Seven*

Springtime

Waiting Cycle

Don't be impatient with the universe—it sure hasn't been impatient with you!

Patience may be bitter, but it bears sweet fruit. ~*South African Proverb*

Springtime

Spirit Remains the Same

When you can't find God, who moved?

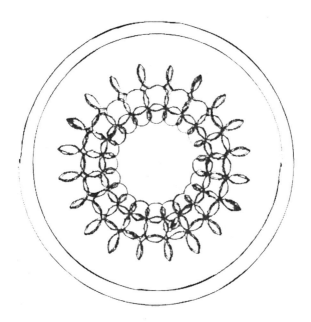

Man's law changes with his understanding of man. Only the laws of the spirit remain always the same. *~Crow Wisdom*

Springtime

Putting Our Baskets Together

We may not have it all together, BUT together we have it ALL!

Naku te rourou nau te rourou ka ora ai te iwi. With your basket and my basket the people will live. ~Maori Proverb (maori.cl/proverbs)

Springtime

Stories

At one of my first meetings, Don H. explained that the front part of the Big Book

is the "meat of the program" and the stories are the "hamburger helper."
~Penny P. ,
As We See It

It doesn't interest me if the story you're telling me is true. I want to know if you can disappoint another to be true to yourself; if you can bear the accusation of betrayal and not betray your own soul. ~Oriah Mountain Dreamer, A Native American Elder

Springtime

Pick up a Hoe

God takes care of you, but if you want potatoes, pick up a hoe. *~Popular Recovery Saying*

When you exert yourself, your God is yours, when you do not exert yourself, your God is not yours. *~ Sumerian Proverb (3000 BC)*

Springtime

Flying Backwards

I recognize that my past is why I'm here
today {...} Those past events brought me down
so I could look inside. *~CDA First Edition, P 216*

Se wo were fi na wosankofa a yenkyi: It is not
wrong to go back for that which you have
forgotten. *~African, Akan*

Springtime

The Message is the Message

Examine what is said, not who speaks. *~Walk Softly and Carry a Big Book*

Respect the beliefs of others.
Listen with courtesy when others speak.
Respect the wisdom of people in council.
~Sacred Earth News

Springtime

Rationalization is a Cunning Fox

We rationalize to ourselves that we know 'what is and is not important, and which fact ought to be lied about.' Thank God our sponsor's ears are finely attuned to the channel of truth. *~Conscious Contact, Dec 14*

If truth and falsehood were pictured they would be represented by a terrible lion and a cunning fox. *~John Wortabet, Arabian Wisdom, sacred-texts.com*

Springtime

Purpose on One

Tradition Five: Each group has but one primary purpose - to carry its message to the chemically dependent person who still suffers. *~Chemically Dependent Anonymous*

I ulu no ka lala i ke kumu: The reach of a tree's branches depends on its trunk.
~Hawaiian Proverb

Springtime

Pray in Silence or Pray Aloud

I just stop and tune in to this universal
energy and am transformed to the level of my
willingness. *~ Ruth Fishel, Time for Joy,
September 20*

My mother taught
me to kneel and
pray to Usen
for strength,
health, wisdom and protection. Sometimes we
prayed in silence; sometimes each one prayed
aloud; sometimes an aged person prayed for
all of us... and to Usen. *~Geronimo*

Springtime

In Our Hands

My success depends on me getting up one
more time than I fall.   *~Pocket Sponsor, Day
Twenty-seven/6:00 AM*

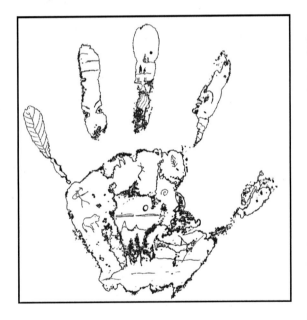

He kai kei aku ringa. There is food at the end
of my hands. *~Eskimo Wisdom*

Springtime

Lion's Den

Daniel didn't go back to the lion's den to get his hat. Don't entertain the thought. ~*Walk Softly and Carry a Big Book*

Only the foolish visit the land of the cannibals. ~*Maori Proverb*

Springtime

Into the Flame

...for thus you will be learning to live. You will make mistakes, but if you are in earnest they will not drag you down. *~Big Book, p 117*

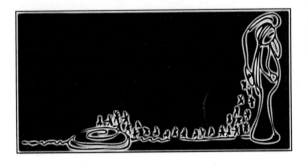

Ignorance is heavy--why be attached to it? It can be cast into the flame. *~Dhyani Ywahoo, Voices of our Ancestors-Cherokee Teachings*

Springtime

Winds of Change

People who relapse usually do so because they accepted the things they could have changed.

Change means that I stop doing all the negative behaviors that were associated with my drinking and drugging. *~Red Road, p 59*

Springtime

Spirit of the Tribe

We shall be with you in the Fellowship of the Spirit, and you will surely meet some of us as you trudge the Road of Happy Destiny. *~The Big Book, P 64*

We know that the Itongo is not the mere Spirit of the Tribe, but is the Spirit within and above all men -- even all things; and that at the end, all men being one in Spirit, all are brothers. *~Mankanyezi (The Starry One), Zulu. The Theosophist, 1927.*

Springtime